PENGUINS/ LOS PINGÜINOS

by JoAnn Early Macken

Reading consultant: Susan Nations, M.Ed., author/literacy coach/consultant

WEEKLY WR READER®
EARLY LEARNING LIBRARY

Please visit our web site at: **www.earlyliteracy.cc**
For a free color catalog describing Weekly Reader® Early Learning Library's list
of high-quality books, call 1-877-445-5824 (USA) or 1-800-387-3178 (Canada).
Weekly Reader® Early Learning Library's fax: (414) 336-0164.

Library of Congress Cataloging-in-Publication Data

Macken, JoAnn Early, 1953-
    [Penguins. Spanish & English]
    Penguins = Los pingüinos / JoAnn Early Macken.
        p. cm. — (Animals I see at the zoo = Animales que veo en el zoológico)
    Summary: Photographs and simple bilingual text introduce the physical characteristics
and behavior of penguins, one of many animals kept in zoos.
    Includes bibliographical references and index.
    ISBN 0-8368-4001-1 (lib. bdg.)
    ISBN 0-8368-4006-2 (softcover)
    1. Penguins—Juvenile literature.   2. Zoo animals—Juvenile literature.
    [1. Penguins.   2. Zoo animals.   3. Spanish language materials—Bilingual.]
    I. Title: Pingüinos.   II. Title.
    QL696.S473M3218   2003
    598.47—dc22   2003060239

This edition first published in 2004 by
Weekly Reader® Early Learning Library
A Member of the WRC Media Family of Companies
330 West Olive Street, Suite 100
Milwaukee, WI 53212 USA

Art direction: Tammy West
Production: Beth Meinholz
Photo research: Diane Laska-Swanke
Graphic design: Katherine A. Goedheer
Translation: Colleen Coffey and Consuelo Carrillo

Photo credits: Cover, title, pp. 5, 21 © James P. Rowan; p. 7 © Kent Foster/Visuals Unlimited; p. 9 © Bill
Kamin/Visuals Unlimited; pp. 11, 17, 19 © Greg W. Lasley/KAC Productions; p. 13 © Hugh Rose/Visuals
Unlimited; p. 15 © Fritz Pölking/Visuals Unlimited

Printed in the United States of America

2 3 4 5 6 7 8 9 09 08 07 06 05

Note to Educators and Parents

Reading is such an exciting adventure for young children! They are beginning to integrate their oral language skills with written language. To encourage children along the path to early literacy, books must be colorful, engaging, and interesting; they should invite the young reader to explore both the print and the pictures.

Animals I See at the Zoo is a new series designed to help children read about twelve fascinating animals. In each book, young readers will learn interesting facts about the featured animal.

Each book is specially designed to support the young reader in the reading process. The familiar topics are appealing to young children and invite them to read — and re-read — again and again. The full-color photographs and enhanced text further support the student during the reading process.

In addition to serving as wonderful picture books in schools, libraries, homes, and other places where children learn to love reading, these books are specifically intended to be read within an instructional guided reading group. This small group setting allows beginning readers to work with a fluent adult model as they make meaning from the text. After children develop fluency with the text and content, the book can be read independently. Children and adults alike will find these books supportive, engaging, and fun!

Una nota a los educadores y a los padres

¡La lectura es una emocionante aventura para los niños! En esta etapa están comenzando a integrar su manejo del lenguaje oral con el lenguaje escrito. Para fomentar la lectura desde una temprana edad, los libros deben ser vistosos, atractivos e interesantes; deben invitar al joven lector a explorar tanto el texto como las ilustraciones.

Animales que veo en el zoológico es una nueva serie pensada para ayudar a los niños a conocer cuatro animales fascinantes. En cada libro, los jóvenes lectores conocerán datos interesantes sobre ellos.

Cada libro ha sido especialmente diseñado para facilitar el proceso de lectura. La familiaridad con los temas tratados atrae la atención de los niños y los invita a leer — y releer — una y otra vez. Las fotografías a todo color y el tipo de letra facilitan aún más al estudiante el proceso de lectura.

Además de servir como fantásticos libros ilustrados en la escuela, la biblioteca, el hogar y otros lugares donde los niños aprenden a amar la lectura, estos libros han sido concebidos específicamente para ser leídos en grupos de instrucción guiada. Este contexto de grupos pequeños permite que los niños que se inician en la lectura trabajen con un adulto cuya fluidez les sirve de modelo para comprender el texto. Una vez que se han familiarizado con el texto y el contenido, los niños pueden leer los libros por su cuenta. ¡Tanto niños como adultos encontrarán que estos libros son útiles, entretenidos y divertidos!

— Susan Nations, M.Ed., author, literacy coach,
and consultant in literacy development

I like to go to the zoo.
I see penguins at the zoo.

- - - - - - -

Me gusta ir al zoológico.
En el zoológico veo
pingüinos.

Penguins are strong, fast swimmers. They push through the water with their wings.

- - - - - - - -

Los pingüinos son nadadores fuertes y rápidos. Se abren paso en el agua con las alas.

They **steer** with their feet and tails. Their smooth shapes help them **glide** in the water.

- - - - - - - -

Se **guían** con las patas y la cola. Sus figuras lisas los ayudan a **deslizarse** en el agua.

Penguins dive in the water for food. They eat shrimp, fish, and squid.

— — — — — — —

Los pingüinos se lanzan al agua por comida. Comen camarones, peces y calamares.

Penguins leap out of the water to **breathe**. They leap out onto the ice.

- - - - - - -

Los pingüinos salen del agua para **respirar**. Salen del agua al hielo.

They stand in the sun to stay warm. They huddle in groups to stay warm.

— — — — — — —

Se paran al sol para mantenerse calientes. Se amontonan para abrigarse.

Their feathers keep them warm. A layer of fat keeps them warm, too.

— — — — — — — —

Las plumas los mantienen calientes. También tienen una capa de grasa que los mantiene calientes.

Penguins hop over the snow. They slide on their bellies like sleds. Whoosh!

- - - - - - - -

Los pingüinos saltan en la nieve. Se deslizan sobre el vientre como toboganes. ¡Fiuuu!

I like to see penguins
at the zoo. Do you?

— — — — — — —

Me gusta ver los pingüinos
en el zoológico. ¿Y a ti?

Glossary/Glosario

breathe — to take air into the lungs and let it out again

respirar — tomar aire en los pulmones y expulsarlo otra vez

glide — to move smoothly and easily

deslizarse — moverse suave y cómodamente

steer — to direct the course of

guiar — seguir una dirección

For More Information/Más información

Books/Libros

Macken, JoAnn Early. *Polar Animals. Animal Worlds* (series). Milwaukee: Gareth Stevens, 2002.

Markle, Sandra. *Growing Up Wild: Penguins.* New York: Atheneum, 2002.

Tatham, Betty. *Penguin Chick.* New York: HarperCollins, 2002.

Web Sites/Páginas Web
NATIONALGEOGRAPHIC.COM
www.nationalgeographic.com/kids/creature_feature/
0101/penguins.html
For fun facts, video, audio, a map, and a postcard you can send to a friend

TerraQuest
www.terraquest.com/va/science/penguins/penguins.html
For photos and descriptions of penguins in Antarctica

Index/Índice

About the Author/Información sobre la autora

JoAnn Early Macken is the author of children's poetry, two rhyming picture books, *Cats on Judy* and *Sing-Along Song* and various other nonfiction series. She teaches children to write poetry and received the Barbara Juster Esbensen 2000 Poetry Teaching Award. JoAnn is a graduate of the MFA in Writing for Children Program at Vermont College. She lives in Wisconsin with her husband and their two sons.

JoAnn Early Macken es autora de poesía para niños. Ha escrito dos libros de rimas con ilustraciones, *Cats on Judy* y *Sing-Along Song* y otras series de libros educativos para niños. Ella enseña a los niños a escribir poesía y ha ganado el Premio Barbara Juster Esbensen en el año 2000. JoAnn se graduó con el título de "MFA" en el programa de escritura infantil de Vermont College. Vive en Wisconsin con su esposo y sus dos hijos.